Upholding the Original Kingdom Standard

by **Jesse L. Radford III**

Clearing the Cloud of Compromise

Upholding the Original Kingdom Standard

Unlock Publishing House
231 West Hampton Place
Capitol Heights, MD 20743
www.unlockpublishinghouse.com
1 (240) 619-3852

Cover design by Wallicia McCaskill

*Unlock Publishing House is not responsible
for any content or determination of work. All information is solely considered as the point of view of
the author.*

ISBN: 978-0-9835468-2-5

Unless otherwise indicated,
scripture quotations are from the King James Bible.

DEDICATION

TO MY MOM, MY DAD AND MY QUEEN

Daddy, I REMEMBER:

I remember the headlights of our Buick Electra on high beam as you stood in that dumpster on the side of the road between Camden and Warren, Arkansas. I remember mama praying under her breath as you tore through one garbage bag after another, in search of that manila folder that housed your handwritten manuscript. I remember the deafening silence of that agonizingly long ride back home. And even though we were very young at the time, Quintin and I somehow understood that all was not well in the Radford camp. I remember your frustration, disappointment, withdrawal and your sadness;... I remember!

Dad, I dedicate this book to you. Your gift, anointing and spiritual insight have yet to be heard on the platforms to which they are certainly eligible. Whatever blessing, revelation or nugget that is received from this work is a direct result of Holy Spirit's leading and your modeling. I'm still learning from you. Thank you for being my first teacher. Thank you for being my dad!

I dedicate this book to the mad scientist of the culinary world; my mother. Mama, your nightly "experiments" and concoctions were easier to swallow than they were to look at. Many times we would ask you in bewilderment, "what is it," to which you would reply, "Goul-osh" or "Mountain Man Surprise!" Sometimes I think that even you may have forgotten everything you put in it, but bless God nobody died or ever went hungry! Clearly, your anointing was not cooking; your anointing was caring and nurturing. Thank you for speaking to the purpose within me. Thank you for encouraging me to step outside of my comfort zone and challenge the process. You "freed" me to be me and for that, I am eternally grateful!

Finally, I dedicate this book to my awesome wife and best friend. Babygirl, words cannot begin to convey the love, honor and respect I have for you and the anointing that is on your life. You've been there through everything! You have been my greatest supporter and my most gracious critic. I could say more, but the rest I will whisper in your ear. I love you more than pork and beans!

ACKNOWLEDGMENTS

To the awesome group of Christ-like Disciples that make up the Upper Room Christian Cathedral. Over the years, your intensifying "want to" has challenged and provoked me to be a better leader and a better man! I pray that I have done the same. Let's keep it moving forward in Jesus' name! Ain't nobody mad but the devil!

Pastor J.

FOREWORD

I can easily recall my first encounter with Jesse Radford. He was a young minister who was charged with pastoring a church in Northern Virginia, in which the founding pastor had died. I had no idea who he was, but he reached out to me during a men's conference that was held at Greater Mt. Calvary. I remember vividly that he said he was "a young Timothy in need of a Paul." He had moved to the area from Arkansas, away from his natural father – his covering, and wanted to be sure he had accountability for the next level that God was taking him. Because I could remember being a young pastor myself, I knew what I had to do. We set up a time to chat and I adopted him as a son of ministry. Since that time, he has allowed me the opportunity to speak into his life and father him in ministry. I have watched him grow and develop as a leader, walking consistently in obedience to the will of God for his life, his family and his ministry. For the past decade, he has pastored the Upper Room Christian Cathedral, a thriving, vibrant, and relevant church in Manassas, VA.

I am excited about where God is taking Jesse as a pastor and as an author. *Clearing the Cloud of Compromise* is a clarion call to the Body of Christ to remain true to the principles and standards that God has established for the Believer. Each chapter clearly exposes the subtle detours that the enemy sets before those endeavoring to move in divine purpose. The pages of this book remind us that Godly standards are put in place to provide a proper framework for victorious Christian living.

I believe *Clearing the Cloud of Compromise* will help you focus your attention more on the standards put in place in the Word of God and less on the compromises that are prevalent among us.

Bishop Alfred A. Owens, Jr.

TABLE OF CONTENTS

INTRODUCTION

God is the God of the downcast and the lonely. Psalm 56:8 communicates that God has kept track of every sleepless night and caught and recorded every one of your tears. He even numbered each strand of hair on your head (see Luke 12:7). These things are important to God because He loves you! God's love for you is eternal, everlasting and unrestricted. Regardless of your past or your present, you can begin to know this love by simply reading, believing, and applying the following words.

PART I

IT'S CALLED COMPROMISE

Samuel also said unto Saul, The Lord sent me to anoint thee to be king over his people, over Israel: now therefore hearken thou unto the voice of the words of the Lord. [2] Thus saith the Lord of hosts, I remember that which Amalek did to Israel, how he laid wait for him in the way, when he came up from Egypt. [3] Now go and smite Amalek, and utterly destroy all that they have, and spare them not; but slay both man and woman, infant and suckling, ox and sheep, camel and ass.

I Samuel 15: 1-3

We are living in one of the greatest eras of human history. Never before have we had as great an opportunity to do whatever, be whoever, and go wherever we choose. What use to be the "limit" has become another rung in the ladder of success and elevation. The things that we once thought were the apexes of human accomplishment in a particular genre have become just another stepping stone to something greater and more wonderful. Records that once seemed impossible to reach, not to mention break, are falling down around us with the regularity of autumn leaves in September. Limits are being tested and barriers are being broken. Custodians all over corporate America (and the sports world) are feverishly working to sweep up the charred remains of glass ceilings. Envelopes aren't being pushed anymore, they're being shoved! Opportunities are afforded us with regularity, but what is it really costing us? At what cost are we advancing? At what cost are we moving forward? At what cost are we reaching heights that we've never reached before? At what cost are the new records and benchmarks being set? At what cost? As a student of leadership, I understand that, quite often, you have to give up in order to go up; but it concerns me, particularly within the Body of Christ, that many of us, in our endeavor to go up are foolishly giving up the wrong things. It's happening all over the world and especially within the Christian Church! In our endeavor to go higher and to reach farther spiritually, there will be some things that we will have to give up in order to go up to stay in authentic fellowship with God, but I am convinced that we're giving up the wrong things.

It's called COMPROMISE! What use to be appalling to us has now become appealing to us. It is called COMPROMISE! What once made us sick to even imagine has now made us psyched to entertain. It's called COMPROMISE! In Psalms 40:8 these words are recorded, *"I delight to do thy will, O my God: yea, thy law is within my heart."* And while there are many within the Body of Christ whose love for God is genuine and sincere -- therein lays a dirty little secret that they would never freely admit -- their Godly delights have changed. However subtle, however non-descript, however seemingly harmless, their delights in the Divine have changed. Don't get it twisted, there is no sin involved yet; but there also is no standard. Before sin enters the life of a Christian, Godly standards and delights are the first to go.

When our Godly delights are deformed, damaged, and disjointed from their original position, everything that follows is adversely affected. It's called COMPROMISE! What does it mean to compromise?

Compromise means to adjust and settle. It is mid-way between two extremes. To compromise means to accommodate. Now please don't misunderstand me on this. I know that there are many things in life that require and even demand the art of compromise. In its proper context, compromise can be a very useful and vital component to healthy relationships. There will be moments and instances where you and I will have to step down and give way to each other to get along, but not with God!

I do understand that as saved and as sanctified as you and I both are, there will come a time when we both will have to compromise some of our ideas, and ideologies to keep peace between us. However, neither you nor I should ever compromise with God! There are times when compromising with one another is the best solution, but not with God. Compromising God's plan always sets another standard. When we compromise God's plan, the "commanded way" is replaced by the "comfortable way." The bottom line is this; God's command and our compromise don't mix.

Compromise clouds the command of God until the compromise becomes the new command! Let me break that down to you. God has told all of us who confess His Son as Lord to be holy. He says in His Word, *"[15] But as he which hath called you is holy, so be ye holy in all manner of conversation; [16] Because it is written, Be ye holy; for I am holy."* 1 Peter 1:15-16 (KJV).

Notice the absence of a time line or set schedule for holy living. According to the Scripture, holy wasn't something you stepped into and out of like a favorite pair of slippers. No, holy was intended to be a matter of lifestyle or "conversation." Literally speaking, God commanded that our everyday behavior and attitude drip with "holy;" "**BE-***have*" **HOLY**! This is the command, but because many of us had some carnal desire to satiate and an irreverent itch to scratch, our compromise suspended and suppressed the behavior and attitude of holy that the original command established. Thus instead of pursuing holy every day, as commanded, we compromise by shooting for holy on Sundays only. Unfortunately, this kind of spiritual compromise happens everyday, in every way, all over the world.

This spirit of compromise concerning the things that God has commanded and plainly displayed in His Word is clouding the perception and reality of sin and disobedience in the church. It has become painfully evident to me that many Christians don't believe that God has a problem with partial obedience, but partial obedience is whole sin! We have never been able to pick and choose what we were going to obey and what we weren't going to obey with God. Jesus reminds us in his discourse with the devil in the wilderness. *But he answered and said, "It is written, Man shall not live by bread alone, but by every word that proceedeth out of the mouth of God."* (Matthew 4:4)

In I Samuel chapter 15, we find the Word of the Lord directed toward Saul, Israel's first king. At the leading of the Lord, Samuel anointed Saul King over Israel and Saul's first kingly duty was to utterly destroy the Amalekites. The Lord wanted Saul to wipe this group off the face of the earth. Saul's instructions were simple; kill them all! Kill every man, woman, and child. God's command was to kill everything! Kill every ox, camel, sheep, dog, cat, donkey, gerbil, and hamster. Nothing resembling or associated with the Amalekites was to remain alive because the Amalekites and God had history! When Israel, God's chosen people, were coming out of Egypt, with clothes still damp from their Red Sea experience, and beginning their journey through the wilderness they were attacked from behind by the Amalekites. As Israel was in transition — moving from one stage to another — they were attacked by the Amalekites. And isn't that like the devil? Just as you're coming out of one thing and preparing yourself to go into something else he attacks you. This attack is not by accident; on the contrary, it is very strategic.

You see, the devil knows when we're in transition we are in our most vulnerable state. People in transition are prime targets for the devil, because we're not where we were, neither are we where we need to be. The devil takes advantage of the fact that transition can often be one of the most shaky and unstable places in life. The uneasiness of the past and the uncertainty of the future is what make transition so uncomfortable. But as uncertain and as uncomfortable as transition is, without it, our spiritual growth would be stunted. Transition facilitates maturity! God's anger toward the Amalekites stemmed not just from their attack on Israel, but from the way they attacked Israel. The Amalekites attacked Israel from their rear. All of the old, weak and feeble folk were found in the back. Isn't it like the devil to always attack you at your weakest point? The devil is too smart to attack you where you're strong; no, he attacks your weak places — your "soft" spots and your "tender" areas. That is why it is so important to surrender those things and those people that are closest and dearest to your heart to God because the devil knows how to use our hearts against us.

Scripture says that, *"the heart is deceitful above all things, and desperately wicked: who can know it?"* (Jeremiah 17:9) If left unsecured or unguarded the devil can use the things and the people that you carry on your heart to hurt, hinder and hamper you! But when you choose to abide under the shadow of the Almighty (Psalm 91:1) in every area of life, it will be hard for the devil to get in. Ephesians 4:27 states,

"Neither give place (opportunity or license) to the devil." Let this marinate for a minute, **"Quit setting a plate for the devil if you never intended him to eat!"** I **love it** ☺

The Amalekites took advantage of Israel at their most vulnerable moment — their moment of transition. God tells Saul to utterly destroy them. Saul was instructed by God to kill everything! Kill every dog, every cat, every hamster, every gerbil, every seahorse and guppy in the aquarium and every ant in the ant farm.

Rip every head off of every Cabbage Patch doll! Kill everything! God was thorough in His command to utterly destroy and decimate the Amalekites because God doesn't play around with His enemies. The enemies of God are only allowed to hang around because it's not time for them to go. The demons possessing the man of Gadara asked Jesus *"why have you come to torment us before our time?"* Even they understood their days were numbered. The devil knows that he has a long standing appointment with God and he's closer than he's ever been to that appointed time.

God instructs Saul to wipe the Amalekites from off of the face of the planet. If you are like me, at one time, you've probably wished you could do that to a few people. However, certain existing laws prohibit the utter destruction of individuals for therapeutic release.

While we cannot physically or legally wipe out those who do not like or care for us, I believe that there is something that God would have us wipe out and utterly destroy— the memory of the incident. More specifically, the pain associated with the memory. God told Saul that He remembered what the Amalekites had done to Israel. The same message delivered to Saul is now being delivered to you. God has remembered what was done to you! Every violation, every abuse, every injustice, and every assault has been recorded and stored in the mental rolodex of our God. Therefore, because God has remembered, you and I can now rebuild, replant, renew, recover, and resume the pursuit of His promises. The fact that God has remembered frees us to dream and hope again.

PART II

COMPONENTS OF COMPROMISE

7 And Saul smote the Amalekites from Havilah until thou comest to Shur, that is over against Egypt.

8 And he took Agag the king of the Amalekites alive, and utterly destroyed all the people with the edge of the sword.

9 But Saul and the people spared Agag, and the best of the sheep, and of the oxen, and of the fatlings, and the lambs, and all that was good, and would not utterly destroy them: but every thing that was vile and refuse, that they destroyed utterly.

I Samuel 15: 7-9

The total destruction of the Amalekites included their king, Agag. Agag's name translated in the Hebrew language means; flame, fire; passion and heart. God's instruction to Saul was to kill Agag. You'll never conquer the thing that's been conquering you until you put its flame out! Religion has taught us to separate from sin and temptation and while this is true, it is not complete. Because I can distance myself from the sin, but still have a desire for it! For many, this is the reason why so many brothers and sisters who go through substance abuse rehabilitation programs often, relapse. Perhaps, this could explain why many criminal offenders who have paid their debt to society end up owing society again by repeating the same or similar offense.

This could quite possible by why those who say, *"I'm sorry,"* end up slipping — again.

Career apologizers and repeat offenders can't seem to break the habit and the cycle of dysfunction and abuse because they haven't put the flame or the passion for the temptation and the sin out! Scripture says, *"...lay aside every weight and the sin which doth so easily beset us, and let us run with patience the race that is set before us."* (Hebrew 12:1)

But how can I lay aside what lives and thrives in my heart? How can I deny what has been so dear to me? The fact is that none of us can do either of these things alone. There are many strong willed people who boast about what they have given up or broken free from, but they often are only talking about a specific behavior.

Typically, these emotional juggernauts that boast of their freedom are really more imprisoned now than they were when they were giving in to the flame. This is where most, if not all "super" religious people are. The thinking is, "I can change my behavior if I just change my habits." This thinking generally works well in the short run. It gives many Christians the confidence to "test-i-lie" things like:

- "The things, I use to do, I don't do no more!"
- "I don't drink and I don't chew and I don't run with those that do!"
- "The devil thought he had me, but I got away!"

All of these declarations are wonderful and can truly be attainable when done according to the Word of God. However, if your confidence to declare statements like these is based solely upon your own ability and will power to resist ungodly behavior because you now avoid the triggers that once set you off, then those testimonies and declarations should be stamped with a "Use By This Date" notice.

Just like milk, they will soon go bad! Behavior modification alters the action and is applauded the loudest because it usually gets the fastest and most visible results. But the quickest is not always the best. Now, I realize that that last statement was tantamount to carnal and religious blasphemy because we live in such a microwave, instamatic, get now, pay later, give-it-to-me-yesterday society, that the thought of delayed gratification might cause the average person to break out in hives. But, however painful and uncomfortable it might be to unsatisfied, insatiable flesh, God's timing is **always** better than ours. His delay doesn't necessarily mean denial. If you think that a change of venue will have any lasting effect in what you do, then you are sadly and pitifully mistaken. Real change occurs when how you see what you do changes.

This change that I'm talking about begins with a "no compromise" look at sin and unrighteousness. You see, unless your attitude toward sin is changed, your reaction to sin won't. You have to see sin for what it really is – the incubator for death and destruction! You cannot play around with sin! Romans 7:13 spells it out for you,

> *13 But how can that be? Did the law, which is good, cause my doom? Of course not! Sin used what was good to bring about my condemnation. So we can see how terrible sin really is. It uses God's good commandment for its own evil purposes.*
>
> Romans 7:13 (NLT)

Stop asking for the behavioral <u>patch</u> and prepare yourself for the much needed attitude adjustment where sin and unrighteousness is concerned!

I don't know what your "Agag" is, but it is time that you KILL IT!

It is imperative that you put your Agag down because Agag is the heart and source of what drives you to do what you do. When you kill Agag, you silence the voice of the passions that placate to your fleshly desire. The bottom line is this; as long as Agag is allowed to live in your life, you are playing with fire! But I want to pose the same question of the Proverb

31

writer; *"Can a man take fire in his bosom, and his clothes not be burned"?* (Proverbs 6:27)

PART III

ADDRESSING THE FLAME

27 Can a man take fire in his bosom, and his clothes not be burned?

Proverbs 6:27 (KJV)

There is no way that you can hold on to something hot and avoid being hurt by the heat of it! As long as you keep the flame of your fleshy passions and desires close, you are all but guaranteed to incur damage.

I did some research on fire safety during my days as an elementary school teacher and discovered some interesting information concerning the science of fire and combustion. I think you'll find that what I discovered then is very relevant and pertinent to what we're dealing with now.

As I researched, I discovered that: Fire is a **chemical reaction** involving rapid oxidation or burning of a fuel. This chemical reaction requires three vital elements in order to occur:

FUEL - Fuel can be any combustible material - solid, liquid or gas.

OXYGEN - The air we breathe is about 21 percent oxygen. Fire only needs an atmosphere with at least 16 percent oxygen. *(Excess unchecked gives way to sin. What we have must have a purpose - i.e.,. time, money, talent, anointing, wisdom, etc.)*

HEAT - Heat is the energy necessary to increase the temperature of the fuel to a point where sufficient vapors are given off for ignition to occur.[1]

---

[1] Taken from the Fire Safety ABC's - The Police Notebook - University of Oklahoma Police Department website: http://ou.edu/oupd/fireprim.htm)

Now, I know that I just got real scientific on you for a moment, but I wanted to supply you with the natural explanation for how fires start so that its spiritual correlation might be better understood.

Just like natural fire can't exist without three vital elements, carnal fires need three vital elements to occur as well. Carnal, fleshly passions cannot exist without the elements of

Fire is the reaction of a fuel source, also called an accelerant with oxygen. The end result is the production of a flame that gives off destructive energy in the form of heat. Likewise, sin is the reaction of unrestrained carnal desire with an opportunity. The end result is the production of sin in our lives.

DISTANCED or DELIVERED?

Opportunity, like oxygen, is all around us and readily available. Most believers who still struggle with secret sin typically try and tackle the opportunity portion of their entrapment. They figure that as long as I limit my opportunity to sin, I won't sin, but scripture declares that,

7 For as he thinketh in his heart, so is he...

Proverbs 23:7 (KJV)

Distance doesn't equal deliverance! I too thought that as long as I didn't give myself a chance to sin, I would be okay. So I threw myself into church work and religious duty. I became "Super Spiritual", meaning that everything I did or said I tried to have a scripture reference or reason for it. Super Religious would be a better term for what I was becoming. And it worked for a while until I got tired of keeping up with all the rules, regulations and self-imposed protocols that my man-made holiness demanded. The fact was that after going through all that I had prescribed for myself, I still wrestled with the desire to sin. I had to learn this lesson the hard way, because we can all find a way to do what we really want to do, even if we're

36

trying hard not to do it! This fight of bondage originates from the fire of carnal, fleshly desires that have not been put out. And the more that we compromise with the flame of carnal desires, the more susceptible we are to getting burned.

There are many believers within the Body of Christ that have compromised with carnal desires and have been burned almost beyond recognition. Left only with the charred remains of what use to be a life full of hope and potential.

Limiting the opportunity and occasion to sin only delays our real desire. Real deliverance and liberty come only when the flame of carnal desire is put out for good.

How do we do that?

Consider these pondering points when combating compromise in your life.

PART IV

ENDURING TEMPTATION

12 Blessed is the man that endureth temptation: for when he is tried, he shall receive the crown of life, which the Lord hath promised to them that love him.

James 1:12 (KJV)

REHEARSE WHAT GOD HAS SAID ABOUT YOU.

When you rehearse or repeat the Word and the mandate that God has spoken through His Holy Word or through a prophetic utterance, you keep before you the direction and the itinerary that God has predestined for you. Psalms 119:11 reads, *Thy Word have I hid in my heart that I might not sin against thee.* This is why it is so important for the Christian disciple to have a personal, daily Bible encounter with God. Daily devotional books are awesome and great to have as a supplement to your own Bible Study time, but never as your main source of daily spiritual sustenance. God still speaks through His Holy Word and often times we have to cut out the middle man in order to get a word of clarity and direction that is free from the threat and possibility of human contamination or dilution.

Even as you read this book; while I am humbled and honored that you have chosen to read what I have been tasked to convey, I sincerely hope and pray that you have not abandoned your spiritual roadmap (the Bible). Any life or hope that comes from these pages you now read came from the pages of the Holy Word of God.

David's confession was that the only thing that kept him from following through with his plan to sin was the Word of God that was hidden in his heart. The Word of God is the script that Holy Spirit uses to encourage, warn, inspire and remind our spirit man to hold on and stay the course that leads to divine fellowship and intimacy with the Lover of our souls.

The Word of God is not just for the preacher, it is for everyone that has named the name **Jesus** as Lord and Savior of their lives. You need the Word of God in abundance on the inside because there will be times in your life that Agag will try to rise up again and consume you.

There have been documented cases of house fires that have rekindled days after they were initially put out by professional firefighters because of embers that were not saturated by the water the firemen used the day of the fire. That is why now, even if it were a relatively small fire, firemen will over saturate the structure with water in an effort to get the flames they don't see. Fire can hide and smolder in some of the most unlikely places and the oversaturation of water is used to get at what cannot be plainly seen.

If you've ever been the victim of a structural fire you know that there often can be just as much, if not more, water damage as there is fire damage. They soak the structure to prevent a flare up. And that is what getting in the Word of God does for the believer. Every day you get in the Word of God you soak your spiritual structure in that which will keep you from having a carnal flare up. I don't know about you, but I need to get in the Word daily because I can't afford another flare up in my flesh! I have to rehearse what God has said over and over and over again in my heart so that the heat of temptation and sin won't dry me out and make me a walking firecracker! So many believers fall because they're too dry! And they're too dry because they fail to hydrate daily. Psalms 42:1 records one of my favorite verses; "As the hart panteth after the water brooks, so panteth my soul after thee, O God."

Verse two speaks to my thought here; "My soul thirsteth for God, for the living God:..."

This psalm portrays a deer (hart) thirsting for a stream of water: WHY? For those who've read or heard this scripture before; have you ever wondered what caused this thirst in this deer? It is my belief that this deer was running for its life because it was being hunted. All indications suggest that it was probably already wounded by a hunter's arrow. So here we have a wounded, bleeding, possibly dying animal running for its life and it longs for water because of all the things that we can live without, we cannot live without water. Water is a source and a symbol of life. The deer was wise enough to know that when it was wounded and losing life, it needed to replenish what it had lost.

Like that deer, many of us have been wounded by the enemies' deadly arrows and we are rapidly losing strength and losing life, but unlike the deer, instead of running to the stream to replenish what we're losing, we concentrate on stopping the bleeding. We focus on the wound instead of the water. Healthy organisms have the capacity to heal themselves. When the skin is broken, blood platelets converge around the open area and form a clot to stop the bleeding.

Rehearsing what God has said concerning us keeps us strong enough to repair any damage our enemy would inflict on us.

One other thing I noticed from that verse in Psalms was that even in the time of distress the deer remembered where to go. So many times when trouble or opposition comes our way, we can sometimes forget where we need to go for help. I am convinced that the reason that the brook was almost second nature for the deer was because of all the time that it had spent there getting refreshed and hydrated at other times.

Real worshipers can still worship God in warfare -- Real worshipers can still sing praises in a storm -- Real worshipers can still manage meaningful service in the middle of messy midnight situations -- because that place has become second nature to them due to all the time that they have already spent there.

Rehearsing and recalling what the Lord has spoken concerning you when faced with the opportunity to compromise strengthens your stand and reminds you of your divine destiny.

Rehearsing what God has said reminds you of the command that God has given for your life. If you don't have a scripture that speaks life to you when you're tempted to go the way of the flesh, I encourage you to find one quick, fast and in a hurry! For me, James 1:12 was the scripture that I rehearsed all through college and still have to from time to time. This scripture literally kept me from compromising any more than I already had and provoked me to seek Kingdom Grade Holiness. I recall responding with this scripture to, very beautiful and very willing, young ladies trying to get me to compromise my walk with the Lord. As loud and as sarcastically as I could, I'd shout, "MUST THOU TEMPT ME"! It often got a laugh but it was just enough to break through the cloud of compromise hovering over me. Rehearsing what God has said might not make you popular, but it will keep you positioned, primed and purposeful for the release of God's spirit and power!

RESIST OLD HABITS

Another way to clear the cloud of compromise is to resist old habits. In the Old Testament, much like the conquests of today, the custom was to take the items or the spoils of your conquered opponent. It was a fairly straightforward custom -- I beat you up, I take your stuff. This was the custom. But in this particular instance of battling and defeating the Amalekites, God gave the command to kill and utterly destroy everything.

Combating compromise requires that you leave how you're use to doing things. Former ways of dealing and doing things have got to be abandoned because they are currently incubating destructive habits that are fostering separation between you and God's ordered plan for your life.

Before Jesus became Lord of my life, I had a real bad vengeance problem. If you got over on me in anyway, I would not rest until I got you back. And my "get you back" always had to be bigger and "badder" than the way you got me. I just couldn't let things go. When I surrendered my life to God, Holy Spirit filled me and really cramped my "get you back" lifestyle.

In cases where I would be looking forward to a fight, Holy Spirit now had me pursuing forgiveness.

Resisting old habits is never easy to do on your own. James 4:7, 8 says, "Submit yourselves therefore to God. Resist the devil, and he will flee from you." The word "resist" in verse 7 is the Greek word, *anthistemi*, which means to stand against or oppose. Try as we may, this is a job for Holy Spirit. Any attempts at resisting old destructive habits are futile without the leading and guidance of Holy Spirit in your life. Holy Spirit is our helper and resident framer of all things godly. He also is our healer and resistant force against all things carnal. He does so by bringing God's will into every situation. Holy Spirit reveals God to us in new and living ways that allow for our successfully abandonment of every ungodly attachment.

RECOVER FROM YOUR MISTAKES

When King Saul kept the chief things from the Amalekites victory, and when Samuel met him and confronted him about his disobedience, the first thing that King Saul did was pass blame.

Instead of accepting and admitting his wrong, Saul pointed the finger at someone else for his disobedience. Have you ever met anyone like that? Someone who would rather cast the blame on someone or something else; instead of accepting the responsibility and consequence of his/her own actions. Unfortunately, Saul had to learn the hard way that the "spoils" of this battle would spoil his current position and way of life. Saul's decision to compromise the command of God clearly demonstrated a severe lack of trust that hindered forward progress and positive Kingly legacy; not only for him but for his family as well.

Don't make the same mistake that Saul made. Compromise always disguises itself as the "best" way, but it is never the "blessed" way! Saul's attempted "cover up", simply "clouded up" his way. Remember that King Agag's name meant; flame, fire; passion, heart. God's command through his prophet Samuel was to extinguish the flame! When Saul covered what he was commanded to kill, he created a smoky atmosphere. The compromise created the cover up - that created the cloud of smoke - that created the confusion and calamity – that created Saul's cancelation as King!

As you can see, compromise sets in motion a twisted chain reaction of events that end up taking us away from divine purpose and destiny. The tragedy of all of this is that it's only after the cloud has cleared that we truly see all the damage our compromise has caused. Again, I say, don't make the same mistake that Saul made.

REST IN GOD'S TRUSTED HANDS

One last point of interest to consider, when combating compromise, is trust. Where there is no trust, there can be no confidence, and when you lose confidence in a person or a thing, compromise and ultimate abandonment are about all that's left.

Trust, by its very nature, requires complete and total reliance upon the strength, integrity and ability of a person or thing, or else it can't legitimately be called trust. In this case it is trusting in the Word of the Lord for your life and assignment.

God often tells us things through His Word or by His Spirit that frequently contradicts what society has come to accept as within "normal" or "acceptable" limits.

Many people who don't have a progressively growing relationship with God tend to think that He is some kind of "ego-maniac," bent on frustrating the lives of mankind!

It saddens me when I hear that kind of talk because nothing could be farther from the truth! God **loves** us! He loves us more than we sometimes love ourselves. God's capacity for love and ability to love is so much greater than our own that I am convinced that we really don't truly understand unconditional love as we should. God doesn't just have love; He is love! Check this out:

> [7] *Beloved, let us love one another: for love is of God; and every one that loveth is born of God, and knoweth God.*
>
> [8] *He that loveth not knoweth not God; for God is love.*
>
> 1 John 4:7-8

PART V

GOD IS LOVE

⁷ Beloved, let us love one another: for love is of God; and every one that loveth is born of God, and knoweth God.

⁸ He that loveth not knoweth not God; for God is love.

1 John 4:7-8

God is love! Historically translated from the Greek word, ἀγάπη — (Strong's Greek & Hebrew Dictionary).

Agape accurately describes the Supernatural, predominating nature and character that is God!

God **IS** the love that looks beyond all of your faults and sees and provides exactly what you need to overcome!

God is love! God **IS** the love that knows what you did, where you did it, how long you did it and with whom you did it. Amazingly, after all of this, He STILL wants the best and greatest good for your life!

God is love! God **IS** the love that recognizes, in the distance, a broken figure that once arrogantly demanded more than he/she was entitled; lived larger than his/her means and stayed longer than his/her character could carry him/her; limping back to where it all began - home. Love not only receives the prodigal back with open arms, a kiss on the neck, a new robe and a ring, Love also throws the prodigal a welcome back party!

It is with this personification of God, who is Love, that our trust should begin! Trusting God, who is Love, with every fiber of our being will combat, dispute, defy, oppose, repel, and withstand the slightest hint of compromise and rebellion in our lives.

Although trusting God doesn't make us immune to the threat or temptation of compromise, trusting God does make us more resistant to it.

When trust in God is established, tenaciously kept and guarded, its value is discovered and substantiated. Any alluring or attracting feature connected to anyone or anything that would or could cause you to compromise your trust in God is tremendously diminished in comparison.

I would be lying to you if I told you that the allure and the shine of compromise disappeared forever once trust in God is established in your life.

Just as King Saul reverted back to a commonly accepted indulgence of military victory for that day, we all can be enticed to go back to what we're accustomed to; especially when pressured.

I can however, with certainty, guarantee you that the allure to temptation and compromise will no longer dominate or control your life anymore!

Trusting God is a day to day to day process that must be actively and consistently engaged by each of us, moment by moment.

This engagement has its origin in how we process our thoughts about what we know about God and His word and what our flesh wants and desires. However, this mental tug-o-war is given a supernatural advantage when we follow what the writer to the Ephesian church advised:

> 23 *And be renewed in the spirit of your mind;*

Ephesians 4:23

Here, we are instructed to renew, renovate, rejuvenate, refurbish, recondition, resuscitate, and upgrade how we think and see ourselves and the conditions around us! I've looked back at some of the things and some of the people I've sacrificed my time, my anointing , my purity and my integrity for and I foolishly ask, "how could I have been so stupid!" Stupidity, unfortunately, is a costly trade-off for compromise. Lowering God's standard for our lives also lowers our intelligence quotient! It's sad, but painfully true. Even though we may not admit it until afterwards, stupidity always accompanies godly compromise!

Wisdom follows God, and when God's standard is abandoned, wisdom is aborted.

> [10] *The fear of the LORD is the beginning of wisdom: a good understanding have all they that do his commandments: his praise endureth for ever.*
>
> Psalms 111:10

Oh, but thank God for a restoring grace! What a mighty God we serve!

There is no room at all for compromise when you are truly leaning and depending on God! Having a complete and total reliance upon the strength, integrity and ability of God clears the cloud and reveals the SON; that is His son, Jesus Christ!

He has been in the same place that He always has been! There is clarity in the SON! There is direction in the SON! There is definition and simplicity in the SON! An active relationship with the SON yields accurate resolution to everything you face in life.

> [26] *But Jesus beheld them, and said unto them, With men this is impossible; but with God all things are possible.*
>
> Matthew 19:26

Trust in the Son of the Living God with all of your might and be sure not to put your weight on your own limited ways of understanding (because for the most part they've all been contaminated with compromise); but in all your ways (old ways, current ways and future ways) acknowledge (acquiesce, agree, allow, approve, certify, defend, defer to, endorse, recognize, subscribe to, yield to) Him and He shall direct your path. This is God's loving promise to us!

¹ My son, forget not my law; but let thine heart keep my commandments:

² For length of days, and long life, and peace, shall they add to thee.

³ Let not mercy and truth forsake thee: bind them about thy neck; write them upon the table of thine heart:

⁴ So shalt thou find favour and good understanding in the sight of God and man.

⁵ Trust in the LORD with all thine heart; and lean not unto thine own understanding.

Proverbs 3:1-5

Dear Kingdom Citizens, God's plan is STILL the very best plan for complete victory in every area of life! Clear away the clouds of compromise and give way to the revelation of the SON in your life!

INVITATION TO THE KINGDOM

If after reading this book your desire is to live free of the compromise of a lowered standard or see clearly through the compromise in your life, then understand that there can be no clearing of the cloud without first calling on the name of Christ! Honoring and obeying the Son of God brings clarity, understanding, peace and liberty into your life, but how can you honor and obey someone you've never met. It would be my pleasure to introduce you to Jesus Christ and give you an opportunity to invite Him into your life. If you're ready to receive the invitation of everlasting and eternal life that Jesus Christ freely gives, say these words aloud:

Heavenly Father,

I believe that Jesus Christ is Your Son, and I invite Him into my life as Lord and Savior.

Thank You for forgiving all of my sins.

I yield to You as I repent of these sins.

Change me as You fill me with Your Holy Spirit.

I want to live for You, for the rest of my life!

Thank You, God, for my new life through Jesus!

Amen!

No longer do you have to live your life as a slave to sin.

YOU ARE A CHILD OF THE KING AND YOU'RE FILLED WITH HIS SPIRIT!

Your life will NEVER be the same, in Jesus' name; AMEN!

WELCOME TO THE FAMILY!

Congratulations! If you read those words out loud and really took them to heart, it is my pleasure to be among the first to welcome you into the Family and Kingdom of God! The words you just read aloud granted you access into the presence of God as His child and heir! These words also granted you automatic citizenship into the Kingdom of God!

The power at work within you to get you to recognize your need for a Savior was and is Holy Spirit! It was Holy Spirit that drew you to pick up this book and it was Holy Spirit that revealed your need to invite Jesus Christ into your heart! This was a big first step in your journey and your growth as a Citizen in the Kingdom of God! From this point on, your new life in Christ begins! You are transitioning from the darkness of sin into the light of salvation and righteousness as a Christian! To make this transition as smooth as possible I encourage you to ask God to direct you, by His Holy Spirit, to the place where healthy spiritual growth and development can occur. God wants you healthy! God wants you whole in every area of your life. When you're planted in the right place (the right church); this can become a reality.

God bless you on your journey to spiritual growth and maturity, and again, welcome to the family of God!

ABOUT THE AUTHOR

Determined to remain relevant and real at all costs, while seeking sound Biblical solutions to the problems that attach themselves to God's people, is what describes the ministry and heart of Pastor Jesse L. Radford III.

Pastor Radford is an example of the young, next-generation leader. As founder and Senior Pastor of Upper Room Christian Cathedral, a ministry in Manassas, Virginia, he has developed an atmosphere that goes beyond "church as usual." He has quickly become a "leader of leaders." Pastor Radford brings a refreshing blend of practicality and passion to ministry that is truly inspiring and motivating.

Dynamic in delivery, illuminating in illustration and affective in application, Pastor Radford is compelled and commissioned by God to present the message of the Kingdom of Heaven with clarity, power, truth and authority. This ministry gift puts before you a Gospel that lives with you, enabling you to better understand God's plan and desire for your life.

Pastor Radford continues to celebrate life and love with his high school sweetheart and "partner in time," Almeta L. Radford and their two children, Jordan Thomas Radford and Sydney Alyse Radford.